A Year of
Baby Afghans
Book 2

TABLE OF CONTENTS

JANUARY

Finished Size: 36" x 46" (91.5 cm x 117 cm)

MATERIALS
Worsted Weight Yarn: 4
- White - 17 ounces, (480 grams, 1,035 yards)
- Blue - 6½ ounces, (180 grams, 395 yards)
- Pink - 4 ounces, (110 grams, 245 yards)

Crochet hook, size K (6.50 mm) **or** size needed for gauge

Note: Afghan Body is worked using two strands of yarn, forming stitches with first color and working over one strand of second color, carrying yarn with normal tension across top of previous row. Do **not** cut yarn unless instructed.

GAUGE: 12 sts and 10 rows = 4"

Gauge Swatch: 4" square
With one strand of White, ch 13 **loosely**.
Row 1: With White and working over one strand of Blue, sc in second ch from hook, dc in next ch, (sc in next ch, dc in next ch) across: 12 sts.
Rows 2-10: Ch 1, turn; with White and working over Blue, sc in first dc, dc in next sc, (sc in next dc, dc in next sc) across.
Finish off.

STITCH GUIDE

EXTENDED SINGLE CROCHET
(abbreviated exsc)
Insert hook in st indicated, YO and pull up a loop, YO and draw through one loop on hook, YO and draw through both loops on hook.

AFGHAN BODY
With one strand of White, ch 105 **loosely**.

Row 1: With White and working over one strand of Blue, sc in second ch from hook, dc in next ch, (sc in next ch, dc in next ch) across: 104 sts.

Row 2 (Right side)**:** Ch 1, turn; with White and working over Blue, sc in first dc, dc in next sc, (sc in next dc, dc in next sc) across.

Note: Loop a short piece of yarn around any stitch to mark Row 2 as **right** side.

Rows 3-14: Ch 1, turn; with White and working over Blue, sc in first dc, dc in next sc, sc in next dc changing to Blue *(Fig. 3b, page 30)*, with Blue and working over White, work exsc in next 14 sts changing to White in last exsc made, ★ with White and working over Blue, (dc in next st, sc in next st) 7 times changing to Blue in last sc made, with Blue and working over White, work exsc in next 14 sts changing to White in last exsc made; repeat from ★ 2 times **more**, with White and working over Blue, dc in next sc, sc in next dc, dc in last sc.

Cut Blue.

Note: Continue to change colors in same manner throughout.

Row 15: Ch 1, turn; with White and working over one strand of Pink, sc in first dc, (dc in next st, sc in next st) 8 times, with Pink and working over White, hdc in next 14 sts, ★ with White and working over Pink, (dc in next st, sc in next st) 7 times, with Pink and working over White, hdc in next 14 sts; repeat from ★ once **more**, with White and working over Pink, dc in next st, (sc in next st, dc in next st) across.

Row 16: Ch 1, turn; with White and working over Pink, sc in first dc, (dc in next sc, sc in next dc) 8 times, with Pink and working over White, sc in next 14 hdc, ★ with White and working over Pink, (dc in next sc, sc in next dc) 7 times, with Pink and working over White, sc in next 14 hdc; repeat from ★ once **more**, with White and working over Pink, dc in next sc, (sc in next dc, dc in next sc) across.

Rows 17-26: Repeat Rows 15 and 16, 5 times; at end of last row, cut Pink.

Rows 27-110: Repeat Rows 3-26, 3 times; then repeat Rows 3-14 once **more**; at end of Row 110, do **not** cut Blue.

Rows 111 and 112: Ch 1, turn; with White and working over Blue, sc in first dc, dc in next sc, (sc in next st, dc in next st) across.

Cut Blue, do **not** cut White.

EDGING
Rnd 1: Ch 1, do **not** turn; sc in top of last dc on Row 112; working in end of rows, work 123 sc evenly spaced across to last row, skip last row; working in free loops of beginning ch *(Fig. 4b, page 31)*, 3 sc in ch at base of first sc, work 99 sc evenly spaced across to last ch, 3 sc in last ch; working in end of rows, work 123 sc evenly spaced across to last row, skip last row; working in sts across Row 112, 3 sc in first sc, work 99 sc evenly spaced across, 2 sc in same st as first sc; join with slip st to Back Loop Only of first sc *(Fig. 1, page 30)*: 456 sc.

Rnd 2: Ch 2, working in Back Loops Only, ★ work exsc in next sc and in each sc across to center sc of next corner 3-sc group, work 3 exsc in center sc; repeat from ★ around; join with slip st to top of beginning ch-2: 464 sts.

Rnd 3: Working in both loops, ★ † skip next exsc, [dc in next exsc, (ch 1, dc in same st) twice, skip next exsc, slip st in next exsc, skip next exsc] across to center exsc of next corner 3-exsc group, [dc, (ch 1, dc) 3 times] in center exsc, skip next exsc †, slip st in next exsc; repeat from ★ 2 times **more**, then repeat from † to † once; join with slip st to joining slip st, finish off.

Design by C. A. Riley.

FEBRUARY

FEBRUARY

Finished Size: 33" x 44" (84 cm x 112 cm)

MATERIALS
Baby Fingering Weight Yarn: 🧶**2**
   White - 16½ ounces, (470 grams, 2,545 yards)
   Pink - 3 ounces, (90 grams, 465 yards)
Crochet hook, size E (3.50 mm) **or** size needed
   for gauge

GAUGE: 22 sts and 18 rows = 4"

Gauge Swatch: 3½ "w x 4"h
Ch 20 **loosely.**
Work same as Afghan Body for 18 rows.
Finish off.

STITCH GUIDE

> **FRONT POST DOUBLE CROCHET**
>   *(abbreviated FPdc)*
> YO, insert hook from **front** to **back** around post
> of dc indicated *(Fig. 5, page 31)*, YO and pull up
> a loop (3 loops on hook), (YO and draw through
> 2 loops on hook) twice.
>
> **FRONT POST TREBLE CROCHET**
>   *(abbreviated FPtr)*
> YO twice, insert hook from **front** to **back** around
> post of sc indicated *(Fig. 5, page 31)*, YO and pull
> up a loop (4 loops on hook), (YO and draw through
> 2 loops on hook) 3 times.

AFGHAN BODY
With White, ch 182 **loosely.**

Row 1 (Right side)**:** Sc in second ch from hook and in
each ch across: 181 sc.

Note: Loop a short piece of yarn around any stitch to
mark Row 1 as **right** side.

Row 2: Ch 3 **(counts as first dc, now and
throughout)**, turn; dc in next sc and in each sc across.

Row 3: Ch 1, turn; sc in each dc across.

Rows 4 and 5: Repeat Rows 2 and 3.

Finish off.

Row 6: With **right** side facing, join Pink with sc in first
sc *(see Joining With Sc, page 30)*; ch 2, skip next
2 sc, sc in next sc, work 2 FPdc around dc one row
below next sc, work FPtr around sc 2 rows **below** same
sc, work 2 FPdc around dc one row **below** next sc, skip
next 2 sc from last sc made, sc in next sc, ★ (ch 2, skip
next 2 sc, sc in next sc) twice, work 2 FPdc around dc
one row **below** next sc, work FPtr around sc 2 rows
below same sc, work 2 FPdc around dc one row **below**
next sc, skip next 2 sc from last sc made, sc in next sc;
repeat from ★ across to last 3 sc, ch 2, skip next 2 sc, sc
in last sc; finish off: 161 sts and 40 ch-2 sps.

Row 7: With **wrong** side facing, join White with sc in
first sc; working **behind** next ch-2, dc in 2 skipped sc
one row **below**, sc in next sc, ch 1, (skip next st, sc in
next st working through skipped sc one row below **and**
through next st) twice, ch 1, skip next st, sc in next sc,
★ (working **behind** next ch-2, dc in 2 skipped sc one
row **below**, sc in next sc) twice, ch 1, (skip next st, sc in
next st working through skipped sc one row below **and**
through next st) twice, ch 1, skip next st, sc in next sc;
repeat from ★ across to last ch-2, working **behind** last
ch-2, dc in 2 skipped sc one row **below**, sc in last sc:
181 sts and 40 ch-1 sps.

Row 8: Ch 1, turn; sc in first 4 sts, skip next ch, sc in
next 2 sc, ★ skip next ch, sc in next 7 sts, skip next ch, sc
in next 2 sc; repeat from ★ across to last ch, skip last ch,
sc in last 4 sts: 181 sc.

Row 9: Ch 3, turn; dc in next sc and in each sc across.

Row 10: Ch 1, turn; sc in each dc across.

Rows 11-14: Repeat Rows 9 and 10 twice; at end of
last row, finish off.

Rows 15-199: Repeat Rows 6-14, 20 times; then
repeat Rows 6-10 once **more.**

Do **not** finish off.

EDGING
Rnd 1: Ch 1, do **not** turn; sc evenly around entire
Afghan Body working 3 sc in each corner; join with slip st
to first sc.

Rnd 2: Ch 1, sc in same st and in each sc around
working 3 sc in center sc of each corner 3-sc group; join
with slip st to first sc, finish off.

Holding four 14" strands of White together and using
photo as a guide for placement, add fringe evenly across
short edges of Afghan *(Figs. 6a & b, page 31)*.

Design by Jennine DeMoss.

MARCH

MARCH

Finished Size: 38" x 48½" (96.5 cm x 123 cm)

MATERIALS

Baby Fingering Weight Yarn: **(2)**
18 ounces, (510 grams, 2,775 yards)
Crochet hook, size C (2.75 mm) **or** size needed
for gauge
Yarn needle

GAUGE: Each Square = 5¼"

Gauge Swatch: 2½" diameter
Work same as Square through Rnd 3.

STITCH GUIDE

TREBLE CROCHET *(abbreviated tr)*
YO twice, insert hook in st or sp indicated, YO and
pull up a loop (4 loops on hook), (YO and draw
through 2 loops on hook) 3 times.

CLUSTER *(uses next 3 dc)*
★ YO, insert hook in **next** dc, YO and pull up a
loop, YO and draw through 2 loops on hook; repeat
from ★ 2 times **more**, YO and draw through all
4 loops on hook.

DECREASE *(uses next 2 sps)*
★ YO, insert hook in **next** sp, YO and pull up a
loop, YO and draw through 2 loops on hook; repeat
from ★ once **more**, YO and draw through all 3 loops
on hook **(counts as one dc)**.

PUFF ST *(uses one sp)*
★ YO, insert hook in sp indicated, YO and pull up a
loop, YO and draw through 2 loops on hook; repeat
from ★ 2 times **more**, YO and draw through all
4 loops on hook.

SQUARE (Make 63)

Ch 6; join with slip st to form a ring.

Rnd 1 (Right side)**:** Ch 5, (dc in ring, ch 2) 7 times; join
with slip st to third ch of beginning ch-5: 8 ch-2 sps.

Note: Loop a short piece of yarn around any stitch to
mark Rnd 1 as **right** side.

Rnd 2: Slip st in first ch-2 sp, ch 3 **(counts as first
dc, now and throughout)**, 2 dc in same sp, (ch 2, 3 dc
in next ch-2 sp) around, ch 1, hdc in first dc to form last
ch-2 sp: 24 dc and 8 ch-2 sps.

Rnd 3: Ch 6, work Cluster, ch 3, ★ dc in next ch-2 sp,
ch 3, work Cluster, ch 3; repeat from ★ around; join
with slip st to third ch of beginning ch-6: 8 Clusters and
16 ch-3 sps.

Rnd 4: Slip st in first ch-3 sp, ch 1, sc in same sp, ch 8,
sc in next ch-3 sp, ch 5, decrease, ch 5, ★ sc in next
ch-3 sp, ch 8, sc in next ch-3 sp, ch 5, decrease, ch 5;
repeat from ★ 2 times **more**; join with slip st to first sc:
12 sps.

Rnd 5: In first ch-8 sp work (slip st, ch 4, 3 dc, ch 3,
Puff St, ch 3, 3 dc, tr), ch 1, sc in next ch-5 sp, ch 5,
sc in next ch-5 sp, ch 1, ★ (tr, 3 dc, ch 3, work Puff St,
ch 3, 3 dc, tr) in next ch-8 sp, ch 1, sc in next ch-5 sp,
ch 5, sc in next ch-5 sp, ch 1; repeat from ★ 2 times
more; join with slip st to top of beginning ch-4: 20 sps.

Rnd 6: Slip st in next 2 dc, ch 1, sc in same st, ch 4,
(work Puff St in next ch-3 sp, ch 4) twice, skip next dc, sc
in next dc, ch 4, skip next ch-1 sp, (2 dc, ch 2, sc, ch 2,
2 dc) in next ch-5 sp, ch 4, skip next ch-1 sp and next
2 sts, ★ sc in next dc, ch 4, (work Puff St in next ch-3 sp,
ch 4) twice, skip next dc, sc in next dc, ch 4, skip next
ch-1 sp, (2 dc, ch 2, sc, ch 2, 2 dc) in next ch-5 sp, ch 4,
skip next ch-1 sp and next 2 sts; repeat from ★ 2 times
more; join with slip st to first sc: 28 sps.

Rnd 7: Slip st in first ch-4 sp, ch 3, 3 dc in same sp,
(dc, ch 4, work Puff St, ch 4, dc) in next ch-4 sp, 4 dc in
each of next 2 ch-4 sps, ch 2, decrease, ch 2, ★ 4 dc in
each of next 2 ch-4 sps, (dc, ch 4, work Puff St, ch 4, dc)
in next ch-4 sp, 4 dc in each of next 2 ch-4 sps, ch 2,
decrease, ch 2; repeat from ★ 2 times **more**, 4 dc in last
ch-4 sp; join with slip st to first dc: 76 dc and 16 sps.

Rnd 8: Ch 4 **(counts as first dc plus ch 1)**, (skip
next dc, dc in next dc, ch 1) twice, (dc, ch 1) twice in next
ch-4 sp, (tr, ch 1) twice in next Puff St **(corner made)**,
(dc, ch 1) twice in next ch-4 sp, dc in next dc, ch 1, (skip
next dc, dc in next dc, ch 1) 4 times, (dc in next ch-2 sp,
ch 1) twice, ★ dc in next dc, ch 1, (skip next dc, dc in
next dc, ch 1) 4 times, (dc, ch 1) twice in next ch-4 sp,
(tr, ch 1) twice in next Puff St **(corner made)**, (dc, ch 1)
twice in next ch-4 sp, dc in next dc, ch 1, (skip next dc,
dc in next dc, ch 1) 4 times, (dc in next ch-2 sp, ch 1)
twice; repeat from ★ 2 times **more**, (dc in next dc, ch 1,
skip next dc) twice; join with slip st to first dc, finish off:
72 sts and 72 ch-1 sps.

ASSEMBLY

Working through **both** loops, whipstitch Squares
together forming 7 vertical strips of 9 Squares each
(Fig. 7a, page 31), beginning in center ch-1 of first
corner and ending in center ch-1 of next corner; then
whipstitch strips together in same manner.

Continued on page 26.

APRIL

APRIL

Finished Size: 36" x 45" (91.5 cm x 114.5 cm)

MATERIALS

Sport Weight Yarn: (3)
- White - 9^1/$_2$ ounces, (270 grams, 1,010 yards)
- Blue - 2^3/$_4$ ounces, (80 grams, 290 yards)
- Lavender - 2 ounces, (60 grams, 215 yards)
- Yellow - 2 ounces, (60 grams, 215 yards)
- Pink - 2 ounces, (60 grams, 215 yards)

Crochet hook, size G (4.00 mm) **or** size needed for gauge

GAUGE: In pattern, from point to point = 7^1/$_4$";
8 rows = 4^1/$_4$"

Gauge Swatch: 14^1/$_2$"w x 4^1/$_4$"h
Ch 71 **loosely**.
Work same as Afghan Body for 8 rows.

STITCH GUIDE

DECREASE (uses next 2 sts)
YO, insert hook in same st as last st made, YO and pull up a loop, YO and draw through 2 loops on hook, YO, skip next st, insert hook in next st, YO and pull up a loop, YO and draw through 2 loops on hook, YO and draw through all 3 loops on hook **(counts as one dc)**.

BEGINNING DOUBLE DECREASE
(uses next 4 sts)
Ch 2, ★ YO, skip **next** Puff St, insert hook in **next** sc, YO and pull up a loop, YO and draw through 2 loops on hook; repeat from ★ once **more**, YO and draw through all 3 loops on hook **(counts as one dc)**.

DOUBLE DECREASE (uses next 4 sts)
YO, insert hook in same st as last st made, YO and pull up a loop, YO and draw through 2 loops on hook, ★ YO, skip **next** st, insert hook in **next** st, YO and pull up a loop, YO and draw through 2 loops on hook; repeat from ★ once **more**, YO and draw through all 4 loops on hook **(counts as one dc)**.

PUFF ST
Ch 2, ★ YO, insert hook in back ridge of second ch from hook **(Fig. 2, page 30)**, YO and pull up a loop; repeat from ★ once **more**, YO and draw through all 5 loops on hook.

AFGHAN BODY

With Blue, ch 179 **loosely**, place marker in third ch from hook for st placement.

Row 1 (Right side): Dc in fifth ch from hook, (ch 1, decrease) 6 times, ch 1, dc in same ch as last st made, (ch 1, decrease, ch 1, dc in same ch as last st made) twice, ★ (ch 1, decrease) 5 times, (ch 1, double decrease) 3 times, (ch 1, decrease) 5 times, ch 1, dc in same ch as last st made, (ch 1, decrease, ch 1, dc in same ch as last st made) twice; repeat from ★ 3 times **more**, (ch 1, decrease) 7 times; finish off: 91 dc and 90 chs.

Note: Loop a short piece of yarn around any stitch to mark Row 1 as **right** side.

Row 2: With **wrong** side facing and working in Front Loops Only *(Fig. 1, page 30)*, join White with sc in first dc *(see Joining With Sc, page 30)*; ★ work Puff St, skip next ch, sc in next dc; repeat from ★ across; finish off: 91 sc and 90 Puff Sts.

Row 3: With **right** side facing, and working in Back Loops Only, join next color with slip st in first sc; work beginning double decrease, (ch 1, decrease) 6 times, ch 1, dc in same sc as last st made, (ch 1, decrease, ch 1, dc in same sc as last st made) twice, ★ (ch 1, decrease) 5 times, (ch 1, double decrease) 3 times, (ch 1, decrease) 5 times, ch 1, dc in same sc as last st made, (ch 1, decrease, ch 1, dc in same sc as last st made) twice; repeat from ★ 3 times **more**, (ch 1, decrease) 6 times, ch 1, double decrease; finish off: 91 dc and 90 chs.

Row 4: With **wrong** side facing and working in Front Loops Only, join White with sc in first dc; ★ work Puff St, skip next ch, sc in next dc; repeat from ★ across; finish off: 91 sc and 90 Puff Sts.

Rows 5-84: Repeat Rows 3 and 4, 40 times; at end of Row 84, do **not** finish off.

EDGING

With **wrong** side facing, sc evenly across end of rows; working in free loops of beginning ch *(Fig. 4b, page 31)*, sc in marked ch, ★ work Puff St, skip next ch, sc in next ch; repeat from ★ across; sc evenly across end of rows; join with slip st to first sc on Row 84, finish off.

Design by Tammy Kreimeyer.

MAY

MAY

Finished Size: 36" x 44" (91.5 cm x 112 cm)

MATERIALS
Sport Weight Yarn: **(3)**
Blue - 19½ ounces, (550 grams, 1,560 yards)
White - 7 ounces, (200 grams, 560 yards)
Yellow - 5½ ounces, (160 grams, 440 yards)
Crochet hook, size F (3.75 mm) **or** size needed
for gauge
Yarn needle

GAUGE SWATCH: 3¾" square
Work same as Square A or B.

SQUARE A (Make 50)
Rnd 1 (Right side): With Yellow, ch 4, 11 dc in fourth ch from hook **(3 skipped chs count as first dc)**; join with slip st to first dc, finish off: 12 dc.

Note: Loop a short piece of yarn around any stitch to mark Rnd 1 as **right** side.

Rnd 2: With **right** side facing, join White with slip st in Front Loop Only of same st as joining **(Fig. 1, page 30)**; ch 5 **loosely**, sc in second ch from hook, dc in next 2 chs, sc in last ch **(Petal made)**, ★ slip st in Front Loop Only of next dc, ch 5 **loosely**, sc in second ch from hook, dc in next 2 chs, sc in last ch; repeat from ★ around; join with slip st to first slip st, finish off: 12 Petals.

Rnd 3: With **right** side facing, working **behind** Petals in free loops of dc on Rnd 1 **(Fig. 4a, page 31)**, join Blue with sc in any dc **(see Joining With Sc, page 30)**; sc in same st, 2 sc in each dc around; join with slip st to **both** loops of first sc: 24 sc.

Rnd 4: Ch 1, working in both loops, sc in same st, ch 1, skip next sc, hdc in next sc, (dc, ch 3, dc) in next sc, hdc in next sc, ch 1, skip next sc, ★ sc in next sc, ch 1, skip next sc, hdc in next sc, (dc, ch 3, dc) in next sc, hdc in next sc, ch 1, skip next sc; repeat from ★ 2 times **more**; join with slip st to first sc: 12 sps.

Rnd 5: Ch 3 **(counts as first dc, now and throughout)**, sc in tip of First Petal (in unworked ch), dc in same st on Rnd 4, ch 1, skip next ch-1 sp, in next ch-3 sp work (dc, sc in tip of next Petal, dc, ch 3, dc, sc in tip of next Petal, dc), ch 1, skip next ch-1 sp, ★ (dc, sc in tip of next Petal, dc) in next sc, ch 1, skip next ch-1 sp, in next ch-3 sp work (dc, sc in tip of next Petal, dc, ch 3, dc, sc in tip of next Petal, dc), ch 1, skip next ch-1 sp; repeat from ★ 2 times **more**; join with slip st to first dc.

Rnd 6: Slip st in next 2 sts and in next ch-1 sp, ch 3, 2 dc in same sp, ch 1, (3 dc, ch 3, 3 dc) in next ch-3 sp, ch 1, ★ (3 dc in next ch-1 sp, ch 1) twice, (3 dc, ch 3, 3 dc) in next ch-3 sp, ch 1; repeat from ★ 2 times **more**, 3 dc in last ch-1 sp, ch 1; join with slip st to first dc, finish off: 48 dc and 16 sps.

SQUARE B (Make 49)
Rnd 1 (Right side): With Yellow, ch 4, 2 dc in fourth ch from hook **(3 skipped chs count as first dc)**, ch 3, (3 dc in same ch, ch 3) 3 times; join with slip st to first dc, finish off: 12 dc.

Note: Loop a short piece of yarn around any stitch to mark Rnd 1 as **right** side.

Rnd 2: With **right** side facing, join Blue with slip st in any ch-3 sp; ch 3, (2 dc, ch 3, 3 dc) in same sp, ch 1, ★ (3 dc, ch 3, 3 dc) in next ch-3 sp, ch 1; repeat from ★ 2 times **more**; join with slip st to first dc, finish off: 8 sps.

Rnd 3: With **right** side facing, join Yellow with slip st in any ch-3 sp; ch 3, (2 dc, ch 3, 3 dc) in same sp, ch 1, 3 dc in next ch-1 sp, ch 1, ★ (3 dc, ch 3, 3 dc) in next ch-3 sp, ch 1, 3 dc in next ch-1 sp, ch 1; repeat from ★ 2 times **more**; join with slip st to first dc, finish off: 12 sps.

Rnd 4: With **right** side facing, join Blue with slip st in any ch-3 sp; ch 3, (2 dc, ch 3, 3 dc) in same sp, ch 1, (3 dc in next ch-1 sp, ch 1) twice, ★ (3 dc, ch 3, 3 dc) in next ch-3 sp, ch 1, (3 dc in next ch-1 sp, ch 1) twice; repeat from ★ 2 times **more**; join with slip st to first dc, finish off: 48 dc and 16 sps.

Continued on page 27.

JUNE

JUNE

Finished Size: 38" x 44" (96.5 cm x 112 cm)

MATERIALS

Sport Weight Yarn: **(3)**
White - 14½ ounces, (410 grams, 1,160 yards)
Blue - 3 ounces, (90 grams, 240 yards)
Pink - 3 ounces, (90 grams, 240 yards)
Green - 3 ounces, (90 grams, 240 yards)
Yellow - 3 ounces, (90 grams, 240 yards)
Peach - 3 ounces, (90 grams, 240 yards)
Crochet hook, size F (3.75 mm) **or** size needed
for gauge
Yarn needle

GAUGE: 16 dc = 4"; 11 rows = 5"
Center Panel = 10"w x 15"h
Motif = 5" square

Gauge Swatch: 4"w x 5"h
Ch 18 **loosely.**
Row 1: Dc in fourth ch from hook **(3 skipped chs
count as first dc)** and in each ch across: 16 dc.
Rows 2-11: Ch 3 **(counts as first dc)**, turn; dc in
next dc and in each dc across.
Finish off.

STITCH GUIDE

TREBLE CROCHET *(abbreviated tr)*
YO twice, insert hook in st indicated, YO and pull
up a loop (4 loops on hook), (YO and draw through
2 loops on hook) 3 times.

DOUBLE TREBLE CROCHET
(abbreviated dtr)
YO 3 times, insert hook in st or sp indicated, YO
and pull up a loop (5 loops on hook), (YO and draw
through 2 loops on hook) 4 times.

SHELL
(4 Dc, ch 2, 4 dc) in st or sp indicated.

CENTER PANEL

With White, ch 26 **loosely.**

Rnd 1 (Right side)**:** Dc in seventh ch from hook and in
each ch across, (ch 3, dc in same ch) twice; working in
free loops of beginning ch **(Fig. 4b, page 31)**, dc in next
19 chs, ch 3, skip next 2 chs; join with slip st to next ch:
42 sts and 4 ch-3 sps.

Note: Loop a short piece of yarn around any stitch to
mark Rnd 1 as **right** side.

Rnd 2: Ch 3 **(counts as first dc, now and
throughout)**, † (dc, ch 3, 2 dc) in next ch-3 sp, dc in
next 20 dc, (2 dc, ch 3, dc) in next ch-3 sp †, dc in next
dc, repeat from † to † once; join with slip st to first dc:
54 dc.

Rnd 3: Ch 3, dc in next dc, (2 dc, ch 3, 2 dc) in next
ch-3 sp, ★ dc in each dc across to next ch-3 sp, (2 dc,
ch 3, 2 dc) in ch-3 sp; repeat from ★ 2 times **more**, dc in
last dc; join with slip st to first dc: 70 dc.

Rnds 4-11: Ch 3, ★ dc in next dc and in each dc
across to next ch-3 sp, (2 dc, ch 3, 2 dc) in ch-3 sp;
repeat from ★ 3 times **more**, dc in each dc across; join
with slip st to first dc: 198 dc.

Finish off.

MOTIF (Make 14)

Note: Make the following number of Motifs using the
color indicated for the Rose: 3 - Pink, 3 - Blue, 3 - Green,
3 - Yellow, and 2 - Peach.

ROSE

With color indicated, ch 6; join with slip st to form a ring.

Rnd 1 (Wrong side)**:** Ch 5, (dc in ring, ch 2) 7 times; join
with slip st to third ch of beginning ch-5: 8 ch-2 sps.

Note: Mark **back** of any stitch on Rnd 1 to mark **right**
side.

Rnd 2: Ch 1, (sc, 4 dc, sc) in each ch-2 sp around; join
with slip st to first sc: 48 sts.

Rnd 3: Ch 4, skip next 5 sts, ★ slip st in next sc keeping
ch toward you on **wrong** side of work, ch 4, skip next
5 sts; repeat from ★ around; join with slip st to same st
as joining keeping ch toward you on **wrong** side of work:
8 ch-4 sps.

Rnd 4: Ch 1, (sc, 6 dc, sc) in each ch-4 sp around; join
with slip st to first sc: 64 sts.

Rnd 5: Ch 5, skip next 7 sts, ★ slip st in next sc keeping
ch toward you on **wrong** side of work, ch 5, skip next
7 sts; repeat from ★ around; join with slip st to same st
as joining keeping ch toward you on **wrong** side of work:
8 ch-5 sps.

Rnd 6: Ch 1, (sc, 8 dc, sc) in each ch-5 sp around; join
with slip st to first sc, finish off: 80 sts.

TRIM

Rnd 1: With **right** side facing, join White with slip st
in same st as joining; ch 7, skip next 9 sts, (2 dc, ch 1,
tr, ch 2, tr, ch 1, 2 dc) in next sc, ch 5, skip next 9 sts,
★ hdc in next sc, ch 5, skip next 9 sts, (2 dc, ch 1, tr,
ch 2, tr, ch 1, 2 dc) in next sc, ch 5, skip next 9 sts;
repeat from ★ 2 times **more**; join with slip st to second
ch of beginning ch-7: 28 sts and 20 sps.

Rnd 2: Slip st in next ch-5 sp, ch 3, 4 dc in same sp,
skip next dc, tr in next dc, dc in next ch-1 sp, (2 dc, ch 3,
2 dc) in next ch-2 sp, dc in next ch-1 sp, skip next dc, tr
in next dc, ★ 5 dc in each of next 2 ch-5 sps, skip next
dc, tr in next dc, dc in next ch-1 sp, (2 dc, ch 3, 2 dc) in
next ch-2 sp, dc in next ch-1 sp, skip next dc, tr in next
dc; repeat from ★ 2 times **more**, 5 dc in last ch-5 sp; join
with slip st to first dc, finish off: 72 sts and 4 ch-3 sps.

Continued on page 28.

JULY

Finished Size: 32½" x 44" (82.5 cm x 112 cm)

MATERIALS

Sport Weight Yarn: (3)
  Green - 7½ ounces, (210 grams, 600 yards)
  White - 4½ ounces, (130 grams, 360 yards)
  Blue - 4 ounces, (110 grams, 320 yards)
Crochet hook, size F (3.75 mm) **or** size needed
  for gauge

GAUGE: In pattern, from point to point = 2½";
        7 rows = 3¾"

Gauge Swatch: 5"w x 3¾"h
Ch 37 **loosely**.
Work same as Afghan for 7 rows.
Finish off.

STITCH GUIDE

> **DECREASE** (uses next 3 dc)
> YO, insert hook in next dc, YO and pull up a loop,
> YO and draw through 2 loops on hook, YO, skip
> next dc, insert hook in next dc, YO and pull up a
> loop, YO and draw through 2 loops on hook, YO
> and draw through all 3 loops on hook **(counts as
> one dc)**.

AFGHAN

With White, ch 213 **loosely**.

Row 1: Dc in fifth ch from hook, ★ † ch 1, (skip next
ch, dc in next ch, ch 1) twice, [YO, skip next ch, insert
hook in next ch, YO and pull up a loop, YO and draw
through 2 loops on hook, YO, skip next 3 chs, insert
hook in next ch, YO and pull up a loop, YO and draw
through 2 loops on hook, YO and draw through all
3 loops on hook **(counts as one dc)]**, ch 1, (skip next
ch, dc in next ch, ch 1) twice, skip next ch †, (dc, ch 3,
dc) in next ch; repeat from ★ 11 times **more**, then repeat
from † to † once, (dc, ch 1, dc) in last ch: 92 dc and
92 sps.

Row 2 (Right side)**:** Ch 4 **(counts as first dc plus
ch 1, now and throughout)**, turn; dc in same st, ch 1,
(dc in next dc, ch 1) twice, decrease, ch 1, (dc in next dc,
ch 1) twice, ★ (dc, ch 3, dc) in next ch-3 sp, ch 1, (dc in
next dc, ch 1) twice, decrease, ch 1, (dc in next dc, ch 1)
twice; repeat from ★ across to last sp, skip next ch, (dc,
ch 1, dc) in next ch changing to Green in last dc **(Fig. 3a,
page 30)**: 93 dc and 92 sps.

Note: Loop a short piece of yarn around any stitch to
mark Row 2 as **right** side.

Row 3: Ch 4, turn; dc in same st, ch 1, (dc in next dc,
ch 1) twice, decrease, ch 1, (dc in next dc, ch 1) twice,
★ (dc, ch 3, dc) in next ch-3 sp, ch 1, (dc in next dc, ch 1)
twice, decrease, ch 1, (dc in next dc, ch 1) twice; repeat
from ★ across to last dc, (dc, ch 1, dc) in last dc.

Row 4: Ch 4, turn; dc in same st, ch 1, (dc in next dc,
ch 1) twice, decrease, ch 1, (dc in next dc, ch 1) twice,
★ (dc, ch 3, dc) in next ch-3 sp, ch 1, (dc in next dc, ch 1)
twice, decrease, ch 1, (dc in next dc, ch 1) twice; repeat
from ★ across to last dc, (dc, ch 1, dc) in last dc changing
to Blue in last dc.

Rows 5 and 6: Repeat Rows 3 and 4 changing to
Green at end of last row.

Rows 7 and 8: Repeat Rows 3 and 4 changing to
White at end of last row.

Rows 9 and 10: Repeat Rows 3 and 4 changing to
Green at end of last row.

Rows 11-80: Repeat Rows 3-10, 8 times; then repeat
Rows 3-8 once **more**.

Rows 81 and 82: Ch 4, turn; dc in same st, ch 1, (dc
in next dc, ch 1) twice, decrease, ch 1, (dc in next dc,
ch 1) twice, ★ (dc, ch 3, dc) in next ch-3 sp, ch 1, (dc in
next dc, ch 1) twice, decrease, ch 1, (dc in next dc, ch 1)
twice; repeat from ★ across to last dc, (dc, ch 1, dc) in
last dc.

Finish off.

Design by Melissa Leapman.

AUGUST

Finished Size: 33" x 44" (84 cm x 112 cm)

MATERIALS

Sport Weight Yarn: ![LIGHT 3]
  Blue - 20½ ounces, (580 grams, 1,640 yards)
  Yellow - 2½ ounces, (70 grams, 200 yards)
  White - 1 ounce, (30 grams, 80 yards)
Crochet hook, size E (3.50 mm) **or** size needed
  for gauge
Yarn needle

GAUGE SWATCH
5½" from straight edge to straight edge
Work same as Solid Motif.

STITCH GUIDE

> **DECREASE** (uses next 2 dc)
> ★ YO, insert hook in **next** dc, YO and pull up a
> loop, YO and draw through 2 loops on hook; repeat
> from ★ once **more**, YO and draw through all 3 loops
> on hook **(counts as one dc)**.

SOLID MOTIF (Make 14)
Rnd 1 (Right side)**:** With Blue, ch 4, 11 dc in fourth ch
from hook; join with slip st to top of beginning ch: 12 sts.

Note: Loop a short piece of yarn around any stitch to
mark Rnd 1 as **right** side.

Rnd 2: Ch 3 **(counts as first dc, now and
throughout)**, 2 dc in same st, dc in next dc, ch 1,
★ 3 dc in next dc, dc in next dc, ch 1; repeat from
★ around; join with slip st to first dc: 24 dc.

Rnd 3: Ch 3, 2 dc in same st, dc in next dc, decrease,
ch 3, ★ 3 dc in next dc, dc in next dc, decrease, ch 3;
repeat from ★ around; join with slip st to first dc: 30 dc.

Rnd 4: Ch 3, 2 dc in same st, dc in next 2 dc, decrease,
ch 4, ★ 3 dc in next dc, dc in next 2 dc, decrease, ch 4;
repeat from ★ around; join with slip st to first dc: 36 dc.

Rnd 5: Ch 3, 2 dc in same st, dc in next 3 dc, decrease,
ch 5, ★ 3 dc in next dc, dc in next 3 dc, decrease, ch 5;
repeat from ★ around; join with slip st to first dc: 42 dc
and 6 ch-5 sps.

Rnd 6: Ch 3, ★ dc in next dc and in each dc across to
next ch-5 sp, (3 dc, ch 1, 3 dc) in ch-5 sp; repeat from ★
around; join with slip st to first dc, finish off: 78 dc and
6 ch-1 sps.

STAR MOTIF (Make 20)
Rnd 1 (Right side)**:** With Yellow, ch 4, 11 dc in fourth
ch from hook; join with slip st to top of beginning ch,
finish off: 12 sts.

Note: Mark Rnd 1 as **right** side.

Rnd 2: With **right** side facing, join Blue with slip st
in same st as joining; ch 3 **(counts as first dc, now
and throughout)**, 2 dc in same st, dc in next dc, ch 1,
★ 3 dc in next dc, dc in next dc, ch 1; repeat from ★
around; join with slip st to first dc: 24 dc.

Rnds 3-6: Work same as Solid Motif.

Star: With Yellow, ★ ch 3 **loosely**, sc in second ch from
hook, hdc in next ch; repeat from ★ 4 times **more**; join
with slip st to first ch, finish off leaving a long end for
sewing.

Sew Star to center of Motif.

SHOOTING STAR MOTIF
(Make 18)

Rnd 1 (Right side)**:** With Yellow, ch 4, 11 dc in fourth
ch from hook; join with slip st to top of beginning ch,
finish off: 12 sts.

Note: Mark Rnd 1 as **right** side.

Rnd 2: With **right** side facing, join Blue with slip st in
same st as joining; ch 3 **(counts as first dc, now and
throughout)**, 2 dc in same st, dc in next dc changing
to White *(Fig. 3b, page 30)*, cut Blue; ch 1, 3 dc in
next dc, dc in next dc changing to Blue, cut White;
ch 1, ★ 3 dc in next dc, dc in next dc, ch 1; repeat from
★ around; join with slip st to first dc: 24 dc.

Rnd 3: Ch 3, 2 dc in same st, dc in next dc, decrease
changing to White, cut Blue; ch 3, 3 dc in next dc, dc
in next dc, decrease changing to Blue, cut White; ch 3,
★ 3 dc in next dc, dc in next dc, decrease, ch 3; repeat
from ★ around; join with slip st to first dc: 30 dc.

Rnd 4: Ch 3, 2 dc in same st, dc in next 2 dc, decrease
changing to White, cut Blue; ch 4, 3 dc in next dc, dc in
next 2 dc, decrease changing to Blue, cut White; ch 4,
★ 3 dc in next dc, dc in next 2 dc, decrease, ch 4; repeat
from ★ around; join with slip st to first dc: 36 dc.

Rnd 5: Ch 3, 2 dc in same st, dc in next 3 dc, decrease
changing to White, cut Blue; ch 5, 3 dc in next dc, dc in
next 3 dc, decrease changing to Blue, cut White; ch 5,
★ 3 dc in next dc, dc in next 3 dc, decrease, ch 5; repeat
from ★ around; join with slip st to first dc: 42 dc and
6 ch-5 sps.

Rnd 6: Ch 3, ★ dc in next dc and in each dc across to
next ch-5 sp, (3 dc, ch 1, 3 dc) in ch-5 sp; repeat from
★ around; join with slip st to first dc, finish off: 78 dc and
6 ch-1 sps.

Star: With Yellow, ★ ch 3 **loosely**, sc in second ch from
hook, hdc in next ch; repeat from ★ 4 times **more**; join
with slip st to first ch, finish off leaving a long end for
sewing.

Sew Star to center of Motif.

Continued on page 29.

SEPTEMBER

Finished Size: 34" x 47" (86.5 cm x 119.5 cm)

MATERIALS
Sport Weight Yarn: (3)
14½ ounces, (410 grams, 1,560 yards)
Crochet hook, size I (5.50 mm) **or** size needed
for gauge

GAUGE: In pattern, 14 sts and Rows 1-10 = 4"

Gauge Swatch: 4¼"w x 4"h
Ch 17 **loosely**.
Work same as Afghan Body for 10 rows.
Finish off.

STITCH GUIDE

> ### FRONT POST TREBLE CROCHET
> *(abbreviated FPtr)*
> YO twice, insert hook from **front** to **back** around
> post of dc indicated *(Fig. 5, page 31)*, YO and pull
> up a loop (4 loops on hook), (YO and draw through
> 2 loops on hook) 3 times. Skip st behind FPtr.

AFGHAN BODY

Ch 107 **loosely**, place marker in third ch from hook for
st placement.

Row 1: Dc in fourth ch from hook **(3 skipped chs
count as first dc)** and in each ch across: 105 dc.

Row 2 (Right side)**:** Ch 1, turn; sc in first dc, ch 4,
★ skip next dc, slip st in next dc, ch 4; repeat from
★ across to last 2 dc, skip next dc, sc in last dc:
52 ch-4 sps.

Note: Loop a short piece of yarn around any stitch to
mark Row 2 as **right** side.

Row 3: Ch 1, turn; sc in first sc, ch 2, (slip st in next
ch-4 sp, ch 2) across to last sc, sc in last sc: 53 ch-2 sps.

Row 4: Turn; slip st in first ch-2 sp, ch 3 **(counts as
first dc, now and throughout)**, 2 dc in next ch-2 sp
and in each ch-2 sp across to last ch-2 sp, dc in last
ch-2 sp and in last sc: 105 dc.

Row 5: Ch 1, turn; sc in each dc across.

Row 6: Ch 3, turn; ★ work FPtr around dc one row
below next sc, dc in next sc; repeat from ★ across.

Row 7: Ch 1, turn; sc in first dc, ch 4, ★ skip next FPtr,
slip st in next dc, ch 4; repeat from ★ across to last 2 sts,
skip next FPtr, sc in last dc: 52 ch-4 sps.

Row 8: Ch 1, turn; sc in first sc, ch 4, (slip st in next
ch-4 sp, ch 4) across to last sc, sc in last sc: 53 ch-4 sps.

Row 9: Ch 1, turn; sc in first ch-4 sp, ch 4, (slip st
in next ch-4 sp, ch 4) across to last ch-4 sp, sc in last
ch-4 sp: 52 ch-4 sps.

Row 10: Ch 1, turn; sc in first sc, ch 2, (slip st in next
ch-4 sp, ch 2) across to last sc, sc in last sc: 53 ch-2 sps.

Row 11: Turn; slip st in first ch-2 sp, ch 3, 2 dc in next
ch-2 sp and in each ch-2 sp across to last ch-2 sp, dc in
last ch-2 sp and in last sc: 105 dc.

Row 12: Ch 1, turn; sc in first dc, ch 4, ★ skip next dc,
slip st in next dc, ch 4; repeat from ★ across to last 2 dc,
skip next dc, sc in last dc: 52 ch-4 sps.

Rows 13-117: Repeat Rows 3-12, 10 times; then
repeat Rows 3-7 once **more**.

Row 118: Ch 1, turn; sc in first sc, ch 2, (slip st in next
ch-4 sp, ch 2) across to last sc, sc in last sc: 53 ch-2 sps.

Row 119: Turn; slip st in first ch-2 sp, ch 3, 2 dc in
next ch-2 sp and in each ch-2 sp across to last ch-2 sp, dc
in last ch-2 sp and in last sc; do **not** finish off: 105 dc.

EDGING

Rnd 1: Ch 1, turn; 2 sc in first dc, sc in each dc across
to last dc, 3 sc in last dc; work 149 sc evenly spaced
across end of rows; working in free loops of beginning
ch *(Fig. 4b, page 31)*, 3 sc in marked ch, sc in each
ch across to last ch, 3 sc in last ch; work 149 sc evenly
spaced across end of rows, sc in same st as first sc; join
with slip st to first sc: 516 sc.

Rnd 2: Ch 3, do **not** turn; dc in same st and in each
sc across to center sc of next corner 3-sc group, 3 dc
in center sc, ★ dc in each sc across to center sc of next
corner 3-sc group, 3 dc in center sc; repeat from ★ once
more, dc in each sc across, dc in same st as first dc; join
with slip st to first dc: 524 dc.

Rnd 3: Ch 1, 2 sc in same st, ★ sc in each dc across to
center dc of next corner 3-dc group, 3 sc in center dc;
repeat from ★ 2 times **more**, sc in each dc across and in
same st as first sc; join with slip st to first sc: 532 sc.

Rnd 4: Ch 3, 2 dc in same st, work FPtr around dc
one rnd **below** same st, ★ (dc in next sc, work FPtr
around dc one rnd **below** next sc) across to center sc
of next corner 3-sc group, 5 dc in center sc, work FPtr
around same dc as last FPtr made; repeat from ★ 2
times **more**, dc in next sc, (work FPtr around dc one rnd
below next sc, dc in next sc) across to last sc, work FPtr
around same dc as first FPtr made, 2 dc in same st as first
dc; join with slip st to first dc: 548 sts.

Rnd 5: Ch 4, skip next st, ★ slip st in next st, ch 4, skip
next st; repeat from ★ around; join with slip st to same st
as joining, finish off.

Design by Jennine DeMoss.

OCTOBER

OCTOBER

Finished Size: 36" x 45" (91.5 cm x 114.5 cm)

MATERIALS

Sport Weight Yarn: **LIGHT 3**
  White - 12 ounces, (340 grams, 1,290 yards)
  Green - 3 ounces, (90 grams, 320 yards)
  Blue - 2 ounces, (60 grams, 215 yards)
  Pink - 2 ounces, (60 grams, 215 yards)
  Purple - 2 ounces, (60 grams, 215 yards)
Crochet hook, size H (5.00 mm) **or** size needed
  for gauge
Yarn needle

GAUGE: Each Strip = 4" wide; 16 dc = 3"

Gauge Swatch: 1½"w x 5¼"h
Work same as Strip Center through Row 9.

STITCH GUIDE

TREBLE CROCHET *(abbreviated tr)*
YO twice, insert hook in st indicated, YO and pull
up a loop (4 loops on hook), (YO and draw through
2 loops on hook) 3 times.

CLUSTER *(uses one st)*
★ YO, insert hook in st indicated, YO and pull up a
loop, YO and draw through 2 loops on hook; repeat
from ★ 2 times **more**, YO and draw through all
4 loops on hook.

FRONT POST TREBLE CROCHET
  (abbreviated FPtr)
YO twice, insert hook from **front** to **back** around
post of Cluster indicated *(Fig. 5, page 31)*, YO
and pull up a loop (4 loops on hook), (YO and draw
through 2 loops on hook) 3 times.

STRIP (Make 9)

Note: Make the following number of Strips using the
color indicated for the Center: 3 - Green, 2 - Pink,
2- Purple, and 2 - Blue.

CENTER

With color indicated, ch 9 **loosely**.

Row 1: Work Cluster in fifth ch from hook **(4 skipped
chs count as first tr)**, ch 3, skip next 2 chs, work
Cluster in next ch, tr in last ch: 4 sts and one ch-3 sp.

Row 2 (Right side)**:** Ch 4 **(counts as first tr, now and
throughout)**, turn; work FPtr around next Cluster, (dc,
ch 1, dc) in next ch-3 sp, work FPtr around next Cluster,
tr in last tr: 6 sts and one ch-1 sp.

Note: Loop a short piece of yarn around any stitch to
mark Row 2 as **right** side and bottom edge.

Row 3: Ch 4, turn; work Cluster in next FPtr, ch 3, skip
next 2 dc, work Cluster in next FPtr, tr in last tr: 4 sts and
one ch-3 sp.

Row 4: Ch 4, turn; work FPtr around next Cluster, (dc,
ch 1, dc) in next ch-3 sp, work FPtr around next Cluster,
tr in last tr: 6 sts and one ch-1 sp.

Rows 5-72: Repeat Rows 3 and 4, 34 times.

Row 73: Ch 4, turn; work Cluster in next FPtr, ch 2,
skip next 2 dc, work Cluster in next FPtr, tr in last tr:
4 sts and one ch-2 sp.

Edging: Ch 1, turn; skip first tr, sc in next Cluster and
in next 2 chs, sc in next 2 sts; working in end of rows,
4 sc in first row, (3 sc in each of next 35 rows, 4 sc in
next row) twice; working in free loops of beginning ch
(Fig. 4b, page 31), sc in ch at base of first Cluster and in
next 4 chs; working in end of rows, 4 sc in first row, (3 sc
in each of next 35 rows, 4 sc in next row) twice; join with
slip st to first sc, finish off: 454 sc.

BORDER

Rnd 1: With **right** side facing and working in Back
Loops Only *(Fig. 1, page 30)*, join White with slip st in
same st as joining; ch 3 **(counts as first dc, now and
throughout)**, 3 dc in same st, † dc in next 3 sc, 4 dc
in next sc, dc in next 2 sc, 2 dc in next sc, dc in next
216 sc, 2 dc in next sc, dc in next 2 sc †, 4 dc in next
sc, repeat from † to † once; join with slip st to first dc:
470 dc.

Rnd 2: Ch 1, working in both loops, sc in same st,
(ch 2, skip next dc, sc in next dc) 8 times, (ch 2, skip next
2 dc, sc in next dc) 71 times, (ch 2, skip next dc, sc in
next dc) 11 times, (ch 2, skip next 2 dc, sc in next dc) 71
times, ch 2, skip next dc, (sc in next dc, ch 2, skip next
dc) twice; join with slip st to first sc: 164 ch-2 sps.

Rnd 3: Slip st in first ch-2 sp, ch 3, 4 dc in same sp, dc
in next ch-2 sp, (5 dc in next ch-2 sp, dc in next ch-2 sp)
twice, † 3 dc in next ch-2 sp, place marker around last
dc made for joining placement, 2 dc in same sp, dc in
next ch-2 sp, (5 dc in next ch-2 sp, dc in next ch-2 sp) 36
times, 3 dc in next ch-2 sp, place marker around last dc
made for joining placement, 2 dc in same sp, dc in next
ch-2 sp †, (5 dc in next ch-2 sp, dc in next ch-2 sp) 3
times, repeat from † to † once; join with slip st to first dc,
finish off.

ASSEMBLY

With White, using photo as a guide for color placement,
holding bottom edges at same end, and working through
inside loops, whipstitch long edge of Strips together
(Fig. 7b, page 31), beginning in first marked dc and
ending in next marked dc.

Design by Jennine DeMoss.

NOVEMBER

NOVEMBER

Finished Size: 37" x 48" (94 cm x 122 cm)

MATERIALS
Sport Weight Yarn:
 White - 19½ ounces, (550 grams, 2,095 yards)
 Blue - 2 ounces, (60 grams, 215 yards)
 Pink - 1¾ ounces, (50 grams, 190 yards)
 Green -1¾ ounces, (50 grams, 190 yards)
 Lavender - 1¾ ounces, (50 grams, 190 yards)
Crochet hook, size F (3.75 mm) **or** size needed
 for gauge

GAUGE: In pattern, sc, (ch 1, sc) 9 times
 and Rows 1-16 = 4"

Gauge Swatch: 4" square
Ch 20.
Work same as Afghan Body for 16 rows.

STITCH GUIDE

BEGINNING CLUSTER (uses one ch-3 sp)
Ch 2, ★ insert hook in ch-3 sp indicated, YO and pull
up a loop, YO and draw through 2 loops on hook;
repeat from ★ once **more**, YO and draw through all
3 loops on hook.

CLUSTER (uses one sp)
★ YO, insert hook in sp indicated, YO and pull up a
loop, YO and draw through 2 loops on hook; repeat
from ★ 2 times **more**, YO and draw through all
4 loops on hook.

AFGHAN BODY
With White, ch 162.

Row 1 (Wrong side)**:** Sc in second ch from hook,
★ ch 1, skip next ch, sc in next ch; repeat from ★ across;
finish off: 81 sc and 80 ch-1 sps.

Note: Loop a short piece of yarn around **back** of any
stitch on Row 1 to mark **right** side.

Row 2: With **right** side facing, join Blue with sc in first
sc *(see Joining With Sc, page 30)*; sc in next ch-1 sp,
(ch 1, sc in next ch-1 sp) across to last sc, sc in last sc;
finish off: 82 sc and 79 ch-1 sps.

Row 3: With **wrong** side facing, join White with sc
in first sc; ch 1, (sc in next ch-1 sp, ch 1) across to last
2 sc, skip next sc, sc in last sc; finish off: 81 sc and
80 ch-1 sps.

Row 4: With Pink, repeat Row 2.

Row 5: Repeat Row 3.

Row 6: With Green, repeat Row 2.

Row 7: Repeat Row 3.

Row 8: With Lavender, repeat Row 2.

Row 9: With **wrong** side facing, join White with sc in
first sc; ch 1, (sc in next ch-1 sp, ch 1) across to last 2 sc,
skip next sc, sc in last sc; do **not** finish off.

Row 10: Ch 3 **(counts as first dc)**, turn; work Cluster
in next ch-1 sp, (ch 1, work Cluster in next ch-1 sp)
across to last sc, dc in last sc.

Row 11: Ch 1, turn; sc in first dc, ch 1, (sc in next
ch-1 sp, ch 1) across to last 2 sts, skip next Cluster, sc in
last dc; finish off.

Row 12: With Lavender, repeat Row 2.

Row 13: Repeat Row 3.

Row 14: With Green, repeat Row 2.

Row 15: Repeat Row 3.

Row 16: With Pink, repeat Row 2.

Row 17: Repeat Row 3.

Row 18: Repeat Row 2.

Rows 19-21: Repeat Rows 9-11.

Rows 22-178: Repeat Rows 2-21, 7 times; then
repeat Rows 2-18 once **more**.

EDGING
Row 1: With **wrong** side facing, join White with slip st
in free loop of ch at base of first sc on Row 1 *(Fig. 4b,
page 31)*, ch 1; working in end of rows, skip first row,
sc in next row, ch 1, (skip next row, sc in next row, ch 1)
3 times, † skip next row, (sc, ch 1) twice in next row,
(skip next row, sc in next row, ch 1) 4 times †, repeat
from † to † across; working across Row 178, sc in first
sc, ch 1, (sc in next ch-1 sp, ch 1) across to last 2 sc, skip
next sc, sc in last sc, ch 1; working in end of rows, sc in
first row, ch 1, (skip next row, sc in next row, ch 1) 3
times, repeat from † to † across to last row, skip last row;
join with slip st in free loop of ch at base of last sc on
Row 1: 293 sc and 294 ch-1 sps.

Note: Begin working in rounds.

Rnd 1: Turn; slip st in first corner ch-1 sp, ch 1, 2 sc in
same sp, ★ sc in next sc, (sc in next ch-1 sp and in next
sc) across to next corner ch-1 sp, 3 sc in corner ch-1 sp;
repeat from ★ 2 times **more**; working in free loops and
in sps across beginning ch, sc in ch at base of first sc, (sc
in next sp and in next ch) across, sc in same sp as first sc;
join with slip st to first sc: 756 sc.

Rnd 2: Ch 1, do **not** turn; (sc, ch 1) twice in same st,
skip next sc, ★ (sc in next sc, ch 1, skip next sc) across
to center sc of next corner 3-sc group, (sc, ch 1) twice in
center sc, skip next sc; repeat from ★ 2 times **more**, (sc
in next sc, ch 1, skip next sc) across; join with slip st to
first sc, finish off: 382 sc and 382 ch-1 sps.

Rnd 3: With **right** side facing, join Blue with sc in any
corner ch-1 sp; ch 1, (sc in next ch-1 sp, ch 1) around;
join with slip st to first sc, finish off.

Rnd 4: With **right** side facing, join White with sc in
first ch-1 sp to right of joining; ch 3, skip corner sc, ★ sc
in next ch-1 sp, (ch 1, sc in next ch-1 sp) across to next
corner sc, ch 3, skip corner sc; repeat from ★ 2 times
more, (sc in next ch-1 sp, ch 1) across; join with slip st to
first sc, do **not** finish off.

Continued on page 29.

DECEMBER

DECEMBER

Finished Size: 30" x 40" (76 cm x 101.5 cm)

MATERIALS
Sport Weight Yarn:
White - 6½ ounces, (180 grams, 730 yards)
Blue - 3 ounces, (90 grams, 335 yards)
Pink - 2 ounces, (60 grams, 225 yards)
Ecru - ½ ounce, (20 grams, 55 yards)
Crochet hook, size G (4.00 mm) **or** size needed
for gauge
Yarn needle

GAUGE: Each Square = 10"

Gauge Swatch: 5" x 5" x 7"
Work same as Skirt.

SYMBOL CROCHET CHART
KEY

○ chain

● slip st

┬ double crochet

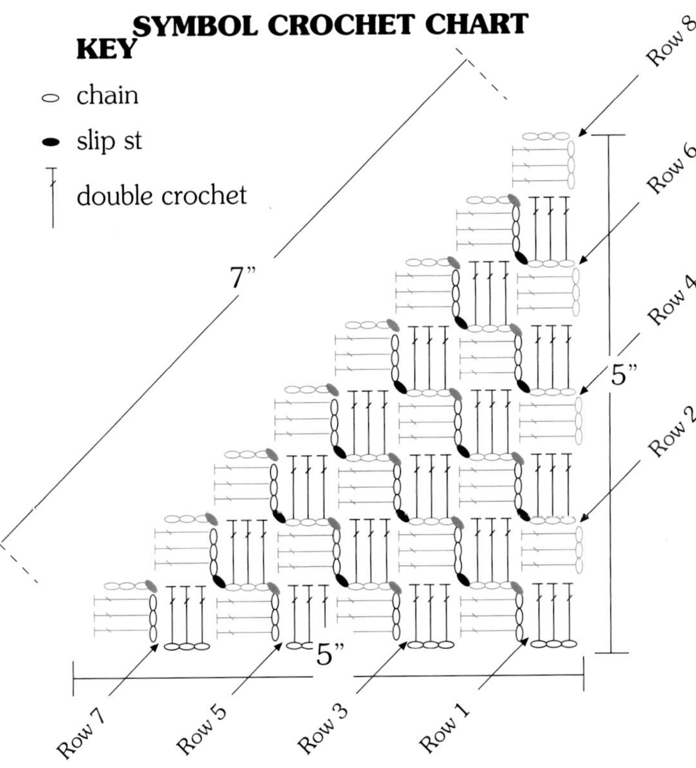

STITCH GUIDE

BEGINNING BLOCK
Ch 6 **loosely**, turn; dc in fourth ch from hook and in
next 2 chs.

BLOCK
Slip st in ch-3 sp of next Block, ch 3, 3 dc in
same sp.

SQUARE (Make 12)
SKIRT
Row 1: With Pink, ch 6 **loosely**, dc in fourth ch from
hook and in last 2 chs **(Block made)**.

Row 2 (Right side)**:** Work Beginning Block, slip st
around beginning ch of previous Block **(Fig. A)**, ch 3,
3 dc in same sp **(Fig. B)**: 2 Blocks.

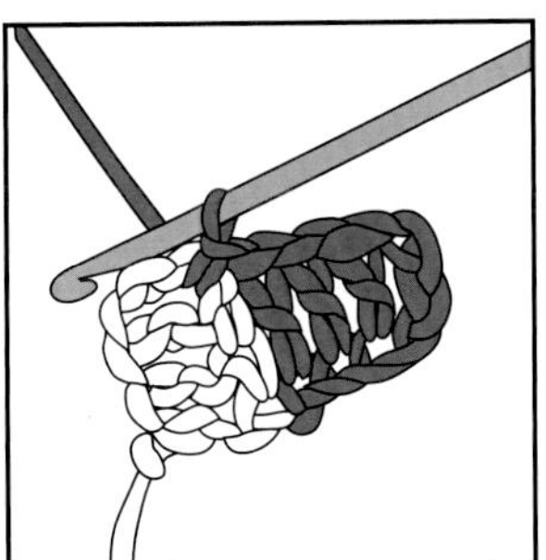

Fig. A

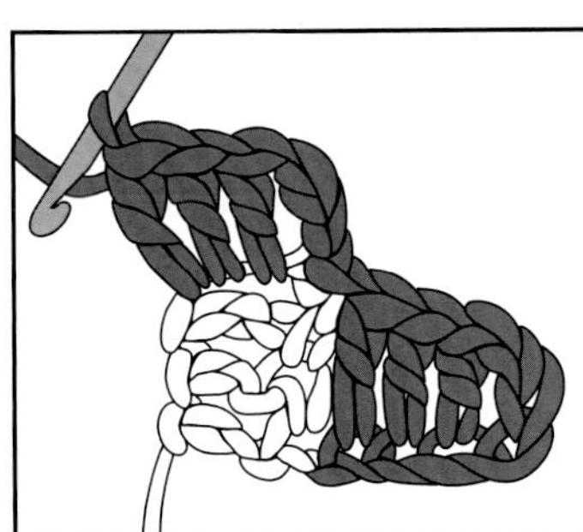

Fig. B

Note: Loop a short piece of yarn around any stitch to
mark Row 2 as **right** side.

Row 3: Work Beginning Block, slip st in ch-3 sp of first
Block, ch 3, 3 dc in same sp, work Block: 3 Blocks.

Rows 4-8: Work Beginning Block, slip st in ch-3 sp of
first Block, ch 3, 3 dc in same sp, work Blocks across:
8 Blocks.

Finish off.

WING (Make 2)
Row 1: With White, ch 6 **loosely**, dc in fourth ch from
hook and in last 2 chs **(Block made)**.

Row 2 (Right side)**:** Work Beginning Block, slip st
around beginning ch of previous Block, ch 3, 3 dc in
same sp: 2 Blocks.

Note: Mark Row 2 as **right** side.

Row 3: Work Beginning Block, slip st in ch-3 sp of first
Block, ch 3, 3 dc in same sp, work Block: 3 Blocks.

Rows 4 and 5: Work Beginning Block, slip st in
ch-3 sp of first Block, ch 3, 3 dc in same sp, work Blocks
across: 5 Blocks.

Row 6: Work Beginning Block, slip st in ch-3 sp of
first Block, ch 3, 3 dc in same sp, work Blocks across
changing to Blue in last dc **(Fig. 3a, page 30)**, cut
White: 6 Blocks.

Rows 7 and 8: Work Beginning Block, slip st in
ch-3 sp of first Block, ch 3, 3 dc in same sp, work Blocks
across: 8 Blocks.

Finish off.

Continued on page 26.

DECEMBER continued from page 25.

HEAD

Note: Wind 2 yards of Blue yarn into a separate ball.

Row 1: With Ecru, ch 6 **loosely**, dc in fourth ch from hook and in last 2 chs **(Block made)**.

Row 2 (Right side)**:** Work Beginning Block, slip st around beginning ch of previous Block, ch 3, 3 dc in same sp: 2 Blocks.

Note: Mark Row 2 as **right** side.

Row 3: Work Beginning Block, slip st in ch-3 sp of first Block, ch 3, 3 dc in same sp, work Block changing to Blue skein in last dc, cut Ecru: 3 Blocks.

Row 4: Work Beginning Block, slip st in ch-3 sp of first Block changing to Ecru, drop Blue to **wrong** side of work; ch 3, 3 dc in same sp, work Block changing to Blue ball in last dc, cut Ecru; work Block: 4 Blocks.

Row 5: Work Beginning Block, slip st in ch-3 sp of first Block, ch 3, 3 dc in same sp changing to Ecru in last dc, cut Blue ball; work Block, slip st in ch-3 sp of next Block changing to Blue, cut Ecru; ch 3, 3 dc in same sp, work Block: 5 Blocks.

Rows 6-8: Work Beginning Block, slip st in ch-3 sp of first Block, ch 3, 3 dc in same sp, work Blocks across: 8 Blocks.

Finish off.

JOINING

With short edges together and using Placement Diagram as a guide, weave Skirt, Wings and Head together to form a Square **(Fig. 8, page 31)**.

PLACEMENT DIAGRAM

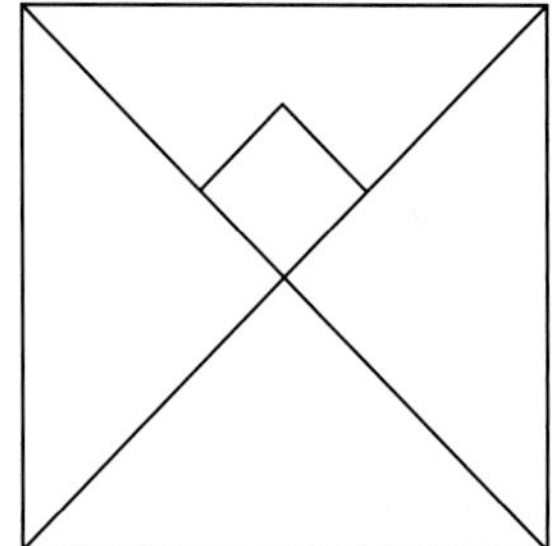

BORDER

Rnd 1: With **right** side facing, join White with slip st in seam at any corner; ch 6, (sc in ch-3 sp of next Block, ch 3) 8 times, ★ dc in seam at next corner, ch 3, (sc in ch-3 sp of next Block, ch 3) 8 times; repeat from ★ 2 times **more**; join with slip st to third ch of beginning ch-6: 36 sts and 36 ch-3 sps.

Rnd 2: Ch 3 **(counts as first dc)**, dc in same st, 3 dc in next ch-3 sp, (dc in next sc, 3 dc in next ch-3 sp) 8 times, ★ (2 dc, ch 3, 2 dc) in next dc, 3 dc in next ch-3 sp, (dc in next sc, 3 dc in next ch-3 sp) 8 times; repeat from ★ 2 times **more**, 2 dc in same st as first dc, ch 3; join with slip st to first dc: 156 dc and 4 ch-3 sps.

Rnd 3: Ch 4, (skip next dc, dc in next dc, ch 1) across to next corner ch-3 sp, (dc, ch 3, dc) in corner ch-3 sp, ch 1, ★ dc in next dc, ch 1, (skip next dc, dc in next dc, ch 1) across to next corner ch-3 sp, (dc, ch 3, dc) in corner ch-3 sp, ch 1; repeat from ★ 2 times **more**; join with slip st to third ch of beginning ch-4, finish off.

ASSEMBLY

With White, using photo (page 25) as a guide for placement and working through **both** loops, whipstitch Squares together forming 3 vertical strips of 4 Squares each **(Fig. 7a, page 31)**, beginning in center ch of first corner ch-3 and ending in center ch of next corner ch-3; then whipstitch strips together in same manner.

Design by Gail Tanquary.

MARCH continued from page 7.

EDGING

Rnd 1: With **right** side of short edge facing, join yarn with slip st in right corner ch-1 sp; ch 6, dc in same sp, ch 1, ★ (dc in next sp, ch 1) across to next corner ch-1 sp, (dc, ch 3, dc) in corner sp, ch 1; repeat from ★ 2 times **more**, (dc in next sp, ch 1) across; join with slip st to third ch of beginning ch-6: 608 sts and 608 sps.

Rnd 2: Ch 1, sc in same st, † ch 3, work Puff St in corner ch-3 sp, ch 3, sc in next dc, ch 3, [YO, insert hook in next dc, YO and pull up a loop, YO and draw through 2 loops on hook, YO, insert hook in next ch-1 sp, YO and pull up a loop, YO and draw through 2 loops on hook, YO, insert hook in next dc, YO and pull up a loop, YO and draw through 2 loops on hook, YO and draw through all 4 loops on hook, ch 3, sc in next dc, ch 3] across to next corner ch-3 sp, work Puff St in corner ch-3 sp, ch 3, sc in next dc, ch 3, YO, insert hook in next ch-1 sp, YO and pull up a loop, YO and draw through 2 loops on hook, YO, insert hook in next dc, YO and pull up a loop, YO and draw through 2 loops on hook, YO, insert hook in next ch-1 sp, YO and pull up a loop, YO and draw through 2 loops on hook, YO and draw through all 4 loops on hook, ch 3, [sc in next ch-1 sp, ch 3, YO, insert hook in next ch-1 sp, YO and pull up a loop, YO and draw through 2 loops on hook, YO, insert hook in next dc, YO and pull up a loop, YO and draw through 2 loops on hook, YO, insert hook in next ch-1 sp, YO and pull up a loop, YO and draw through 2 loops on hook, YO and draw through all 4 loops on hook, ch 3] across to next corner ch-3 sp †, sc in next dc, repeat from † to † once; join with slip st to first sc, finish off.

Design by Carol Decker.

MAY *continued from page 11.*

ASSEMBLY

With Blue, using Placement Diagram as a guide and working through **both** loops, whipstitch Squares together forming 9 vertical strips of 11 Squares each *(Fig. 7a, page 31)*, beginning in center ch of first corner ch-3 and ending in center ch of next corner ch-3; then whipstitch strips together in same manner.

PLACEMENT DIAGRAM

A	B	A	B	A	B	A	B	A
B	A	B	A	B	A	B	A	B
A	B	A	B	A	B	A	B	A
B	A	B	A	B	A	B	A	B
A	B	A	B	A	B	A	B	A
B	A	B	A	B	A	B	A	B
A	B	A	B	A	B	A	B	A
B	A	B	A	B	A	B	A	B
A	B	A	B	A	B	A	B	A
B	A	B	A	B	A	B	A	B
A	B	A	B	A	B	A	B	A

EDGING

Rnd 1: With **right** side facing, join Blue with sc in any corner ch-3 sp; ch 2, sc in same sp, ★ † ch 1, skip next dc, sc in next dc, ch 1, (sc in next ch-1 sp, ch 1, skip next dc, sc in next dc, ch 1) 3 times, [(sc in next sp, ch 1) twice, skip next dc, sc in next dc, ch 1, (sc in next ch-1 sp, ch 1, skip next dc, sc in next dc, ch 1) 3 times] across to next corner ch-3 sp †, (sc, ch 2, sc) in corner ch-3 sp; repeat from ★ 2 times **more**, then repeat from † to † once; join with slip st to first sc: 360 sps.

Rnd 2: Slip st in first ch-2 sp, ch 1, (sc, ch 2, sc) in same sp, ch 1, (sc in next ch-1 sp, ch 1) across to next corner ch-2 sp, ★ (sc, ch 2, sc) in corner ch-2 sp, ch 1, (sc in next ch-1 sp, ch 1) across to next corner ch-2 sp; repeat from ★ 2 times **more**; join with slip st to first sc: 364 sps.

Rnd 3: Slip st in first ch-2 sp, ch 3, (2 dc, ch 3, 3 dc) in same sp, ch 1, skip next ch-1 sp, (3 dc in next ch-1 sp, ch 1, skip next ch-1 sp) across to next corner ch-2 sp, ★ (3 dc, ch 3, 3 dc) in corner ch-2 sp, ch 1, skip next ch-1 sp, (3 dc in next ch-1 sp, ch 1, skip next ch-1 sp) across to next corner ch-2 sp; repeat from ★ 2 times **more**; join with slip st to first dc, finish off.

Rnd 4: With **right** side facing, join White with slip st in any corner ch-3 sp; ch 3, (2 dc, ch 3, 3 dc) in same sp, ch 1, (3 dc in next ch-1 sp, ch 1) across to next corner ch-3 sp, ★ (3 dc, ch 3, 3 dc) in corner ch-3 sp, ch 1, (3 dc in next ch-1 sp, ch 1) across to next corner ch-3 sp; repeat from ★ 2 times **more**; join with slip st to first dc.

Rnd 5: Slip st in next 2 dc and in next ch-3 sp, ch 3, (2 dc, ch 3, 3 dc) in same sp, ch 1, (3 dc in next ch-1 sp, ch 1) across to next corner ch-3 sp, ★ (3 dc, ch 3, 3 dc) in corner ch-3 sp, ch 1, (3 dc in next ch-1 sp, ch 1) across to next corner ch-3 sp; repeat from ★ 2 times **more**; join with slip st to first dc.

Rnd 6: Slip st in next 2 dc, ★ (slip st, ch 3, dc in third ch from hook, ch 1, slip st) in next ch-3 sp, ch 3, dc in third ch from hook, (slip st in next ch-1 sp, ch 3, dc in third ch from hook) across to next corner ch-3 sp; repeat from ★ around; join with slip st to slip st at base of beginning ch-3, finish off.

Design by Anne Halliday.

JUNE *continued from page 13.*

ASSEMBLY

With White, using Placement Diagram as a guide and working through **both** loops of **both** pieces, whipstitch Motifs together forming 2 horizontal strips of 2 Motifs each and 2 vertical strips of 5 Motifs each *(Fig. 7a, page 31)*, beginning in center ch of first corner ch-3 and ending in center ch of next corner ch-3.

Whipstitch horizontal strips to short ends of Center Panel; then whipstitch vertical strips to long ends of Center Panel and horizontal strips in same manner.

PLACEMENT DIAGRAM

● Point A

Pink	Yellow	Blue	Peach
Green			Green
Peach	Center Panel		Pink
Blue			Yellow
Yellow	Pink	Green	Blue

EDGING

Rnd 1: With **right** side facing, join White with slip st in corner ch-3 sp at Point A; ch 6 **(counts as first dc plus ch 3, now and throughout)**, 2 dc in same sp, † work 83 dc evenly spaced across to next corner ch-3 sp, (2 dc, ch 3, 2 dc) in corner ch-3 sp, work 101 dc evenly spaced across to next corner ch-3 sp †, (2 dc, ch 3, 2 dc) in corner ch-3 sp, repeat from † to † once, dc in same sp as first dc; join with slip st to first dc: 384 dc.

Rnds 2 and 3: Slip st in first corner ch-3 sp, ch 6, 2 dc in same sp, dc in each dc across to next corner ch-3 sp, ★ (2 dc, ch 3, 2 dc) in corner ch-3 sp, dc in each dc across to next corner ch-3 sp; repeat from ★ 2 times **more**, dc in same sp as first dc; join with slip st to first dc: 416 dc and 4 ch-3 sps.

Rnd 4: Slip st in first corner ch-3 sp, ch 3, (4 dc, ch 3, 5 dc) in same sp, skip next 2 dc, sc in next dc, skip next 2 dc, (work Shell in next dc, skip next 2 dc, sc in next dc, skip next 2 dc) across to next corner ch-3 sp, ★ (5 dc, ch 3, 5 dc) in corner ch-3 sp, skip next 2 dc, sc in next dc, skip next 2 dc, (work Shell in next dc, skip next 2 dc, sc in next dc, skip next 2 dc) across to next corner ch-3 sp; repeat from ★ 2 times **more**; join with slip st to first dc, finish off: 70 sc and 70 sps.

Rnd 5: With **right** side facing, join Blue with slip st in any corner ch-3 sp; ch 3, (4 dc, ch 3, 5 dc) in same sp, skip next 5 dc, dtr in next sc, ★ (work Shell in next ch-2 sp, skip next 4 dc, dtr in next sc) across to next corner ch-3 sp, (5 dc, ch 3, 5 dc) in corner ch-3 sp, skip next 5 dc, dtr in next sc; repeat from ★ 2 times **more**, (work Shell in next ch-2 sp, skip next 4 dc, dtr in next sc) across; join with slip st to first dc, finish off.

Rnd 6: With **right** side facing, join White with slip st in any corner ch-3 sp; ch 3, (4 dc, ch 3, 5 dc) in same sp, skip next 5 dc, dtr in next dtr, ★ (work Shell in next ch-2 sp, skip next 4 dc, dtr in next dtr) across to next corner ch-3 sp, (5 dc, ch 3, 5 dc) in corner ch-3 sp, skip next 5 dc, dtr in next dtr; repeat from ★ 2 times **more**, (work Shell in next ch-2 sp, skip next 4 dc, dtr in next dtr) across; join with slip st to first dc, finish off.

Rnd 7: With **right** side facing, join Yellow with slip st in any corner ch-3 sp; ch 3, (4 dc, ch 3, 5 dc) in same sp, ★ † skip next 5 dc, dtr in sp **before** next dtr, ch 2, dtr in sp **before** next dc, work Shell in next ch-2 sp, (skip next 4 dc, dtr in next dtr, work Shell in next ch-2 sp) across to last dtr before next corner ch-3 sp, skip next 4 dc, dtr in sp **before** next dtr, ch 2, dtr in sp **before** next dc †, (5 dc, ch 3, 5 dc) in corner ch-3 sp; repeat from ★ 2 times **more**, then repeat from † to † once; join with slip st to first dc, finish off: 78 dtr and 78 sps.

Rnd 8: With **right** side facing, join White with slip st in any corner ch-3 sp; ch 3, (4 dc, ch 3, 5 dc) in same sp, ★ † skip next 5 dc, dtr in next dtr, ch 2, dtr in next ch-2 sp, ch 2, dtr in next dtr, (work Shell in next ch-2 sp, skip next 4 dc, dtr in next dtr) across to within one dtr of next corner ch-3 sp, ch 2, dtr in next ch-2 sp, ch 2, dtr in next dtr †, (5 dc, ch 3, 5 dc) in corner ch-3 sp; repeat from ★ 2 times **more**, then repeat from † to † once; join with slip st to first dc, finish off: 86 dtr and 86 sps.

Rnd 9: With **right** side facing, join Pink with slip st in any corner ch-3 sp; ch 3, (4 dc, ch 3, 5 dc) in same sp, ★ † skip next 5 dc, dtr in next dtr, ch 2, (dtr in next ch-2 sp, ch 2) twice, dtr in next dtr, (work Shell in next ch-2 sp, skip next 4 dc, dtr in next dtr) across to within 2 dtr of next corner ch-3 sp, ch 2, (dtr in next ch-2 sp, ch 2) twice, dtr in next dtr †, (5 dc, ch 3, 5 dc) in corner ch-3 sp; repeat from ★ 2 times **more**, then repeat from † to † once; join with slip st to first dc, finish off: 94 dtr and 94 sps.

Rnd 10: With **right** side facing, join White with slip st in any corner ch-3 sp; ch 3, (4 dc, ch 3, 5 dc) in same sp, ★ † skip next 5 dc, dtr in next dtr, ch 2, (dtr in next ch-2 sp, ch 2) 3 times, dtr in next dtr, (work Shell in next ch-2 sp, skip next 4 dc, dtr in next dtr) across to within 3 dtr of next corner ch-3 sp, ch 2, (dtr in next ch-2 sp, ch 2) 3 times, dtr in next dtr †, (5 dc, ch 3, 5 dc) in corner ch-3 sp; repeat from ★ 2 times **more**, then repeat from † to † once; join with slip st to first dc, finish off: 102 dtr and 102 sps.

Rnd 11: With **right** side facing, join Green with slip st in any corner ch-3 sp; ch 3, (4 dc, ch 3, 5 dc) in same sp, ★ † skip next 5 dc, dtr in next dtr, ch 2, (dtr in next ch-2 sp, ch 2) 4 times, dtr in next dtr, (work Shell in next ch-2 sp, skip next 4 dc, dtr in next dtr) across to within 4 dtr of next corner ch-3 sp, ch 2, (dtr in next ch-2 sp, ch 2) 4 times, dtr in next dtr †, (5 dc, ch 3, 5 dc) in corner ch-3 sp; repeat from ★ 2 times **more**, then repeat from † to † once; join with slip st to first dc, finish off: 110 dtr and 110 sps.

Rnd 12: With **right** side facing, join White with slip st in any corner ch-3 sp; ch 3, (4 dc, ch 3, 5 dc) in same sp, ★ † skip next 5 dc, dtr in next dtr, ch 2, (dtr in next ch-2 sp, ch 2) 5 times, dtr in next dtr, (work Shell in next ch-2 sp, skip next 4 dc, dtr in next dtr) across to within 5 dtr of next corner ch-3 sp, ch 2, (dtr in next ch-2 sp, ch 2) 5 times, dtr in next dtr †, (5 dc, ch 3, 5 dc) in corner ch-3 sp; repeat from ★ 2 times **more**, then repeat from † to † once; join with slip st to first dc, finish off: 118 dtr and 118 sps.

Rnd 13: With **right** side facing, join Peach with slip st in any corner ch-3 sp; ch 3, (4 dc, ch 3, 5 dc) in same sp, ★ † skip next 5 dc, dtr in next dtr, ch 2, (dtr in next ch-2 sp, ch 2) 6 times, dtr in next dtr, (work Shell in next ch-2 sp, skip next 4 dc, dtr in next dtr) across to within 6 dtr of next corner ch-3 sp, ch 2, (dtr in next ch-2 sp, ch 2) 6 times, dtr in next dtr †, (5 dc, ch 3, 5 dc) in corner ch-3 sp; repeat from ★ 2 times **more**, then repeat from † to † once; join with slip st to first dc, finish off: 126 dtr and 126 sps.

Rnd 14: With **right** side facing, join White with slip st in any corner ch-3 sp; ch 3, (4 dc, ch 3, 5 dc) in same sp, ★ † skip next 5 dc, dtr in next dtr, ch 2, (dtr in next ch-2 sp, ch 2) 7 times, dtr in next dtr, (work Shell in next ch-2 sp, skip next 4 dc, dtr in next dtr) across to within 7 dtr of next corner ch-3 sp, ch 2, (dtr in next ch-2 sp, ch 2) 7 times, dtr in next dtr †, (5 dc, ch 3, 5 dc) in corner ch-3 sp; repeat from ★ 2 times **more**, then repeat from † to † once; join with slip st to first dc, finish off.

Design by Cynthia Jaderquist.

AUGUST *continued from page 17.*

ASSEMBLY

With Blue, using Placement Diagram as a guide and working through **both** loops of each st on **both** pieces, whipstitch Motifs together forming 7 vertical strips *(Fig. 7a, page 31)*, beginning in ch of first corner and ending in ch of next corner; then whipstitch strips together in same manner.

PLACEMENT DIAGRAM

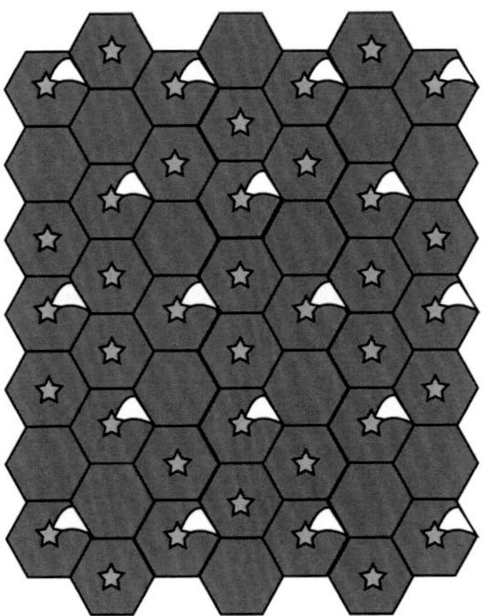

KEY

 - **Solid Motif**

 - **Star Motif**

 - **Shooting Star Motif**

Design by Sarah J. Green.

NOVEMBER *continued from page 23.*

Rnd 5: Slip st in first corner ch-3 sp, work (Beginning Cluster, ch 2, Cluster) in same sp, ch 1, ★ (work Cluster in next ch-1 sp, ch 1) across to next corner ch-3 sp, work (Cluster, ch 2, Cluster) in corner ch-3 sp, ch 1; repeat from ★ 2 times **more**, (work Cluster in next ch-1 sp, ch 1) across; join with slip st to top of Beginning Cluster: 386 Clusters and 386 sps.

Rnd 6: Slip st in first corner ch-2 sp, ch 1, (sc, ch 1) twice in same sp, ★ (sc in next ch-1 sp, ch 1) across to next corner ch-2 sp, (sc, ch 1) twice in corner ch-2 sp; repeat from ★ 2 times **more**, (sc in next ch-1 sp, ch 1) across; join with slip st to first sc, finish off.

Design by Katherine Satterfield.

GENERAL INSTRUCTIONS

ABBREVIATIONS

ch(s)	chain(s)
dc	double crochet(s)
dtr	double treble crochet(s)
exsc	extended single crochet(s)
FPdc	Front Post double crochet(s)
FPtr	Front Post treble crochet(s)
hdc	half double crochet(s)
mm	millimeters
Rnd(s)	Round(s)
sc	single crochet(s)
sp(s)	space(s)
st(s)	stitch(es)
tr	treble crochet(s)
YO	yarn over

★ — work instructions following ★ as many **more** times as indicated in addition to the first time.

† to † — work all instructions from first † to second † **as many** times as specified.

( ) or [ ] — work enclosed instructions **as many** times as specified by the number immediately following **or** work all enclosed instructions in the stitch or space indicated **or** contains explanatory remarks.

colon (:) — the number(s) given after a colon at the end of a row or round denote(s) the number of stitches you should have on that row or round.

GAUGE

Exact gauge is **essential** for proper size. Before beginning your project, make the sample swatch given in the individual instructions in the yarn and hook specified. After completing the swatch, measure it, counting your stitches and rows carefully. If your swatch is larger or smaller than specified, **make another, changing hook size to get the correct gauge**. Keep trying until you find the size hook that will give you the specified gauge.

JOINING WITH SC

When instructed to join with sc, begin with a slip knot on hook. Insert hook in stitch or space indicated, YO and pull up a loop, YO and draw through both loops on hook.

BACK OR FRONT LOOP ONLY

Work only in loop(s) indicated by arrow *(Fig. 1)*.

Fig. 1

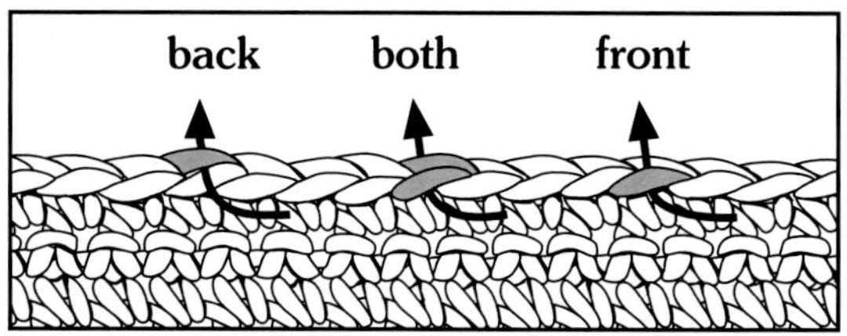

BACK RIDGE

Work only in loops indicated by arrows *(Fig. 2)*.

Fig. 2

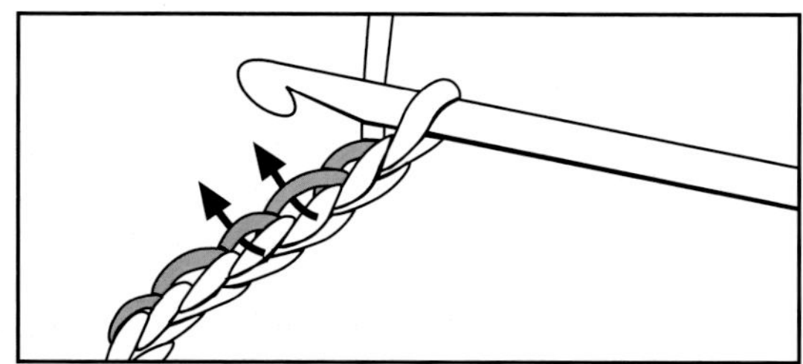

CHANGING COLORS

Work the last stitch to within one step of completion, hook new yarn *(Fig. 3a or 3b)* and draw through all loops on hook. Do **not** cut old yarn unless otherwise specified.

Fig. 3a

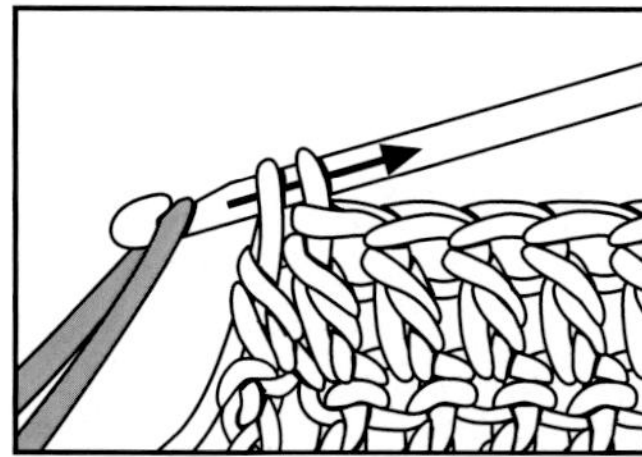

Fig. 3b

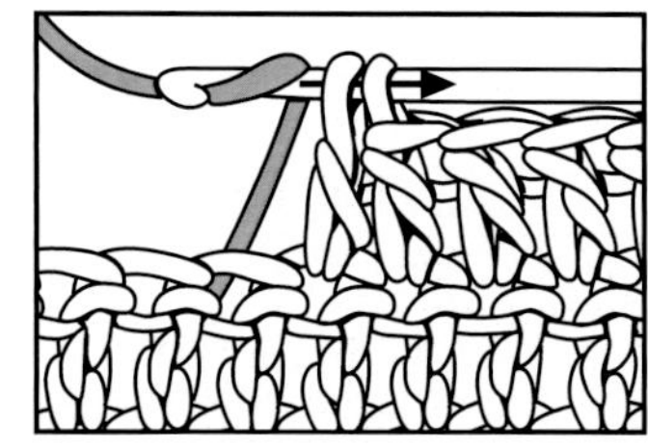

CROCHET TERMINOLOGY	
UNITED STATES	**INTERNATIONAL**
slip stitch (slip st)	= single crochet (sc)
single crochet (sc)	= double crochet (dc)
half double crochet (hdc)	= half treble crochet (htr)
double crochet (dc)	= treble crochet (tr)
treble crochet (tr)	= double treble crochet (dtr)
double treble crochet (dtr)	= triple treble crochet (ttr)
skip	= miss

ALUMINUM CROCHET HOOKS												
U.S.	B-1	C-2	D-3	E-4	F-5	G-6	H-8	I-9	J-10	K-10½	N	P	Q
Metric - mm	2.25	2.75	3.25	3.50	3.75	4.00	5.00	5.50	6.00	6.50	9.00	10.00	15.00

FREE LOOPS

After working in Back or Front Loops Only on a row or round, there will be a ridge of unused loops. These are called the free loops. Later, when instructed to work in the free loops of the same row or round, work in these loops *(Fig. 4a)*.

When instructed to work in free loops of a chain, work in loop indicated by arrow *(Fig. 4b)*.

Fig. 4a

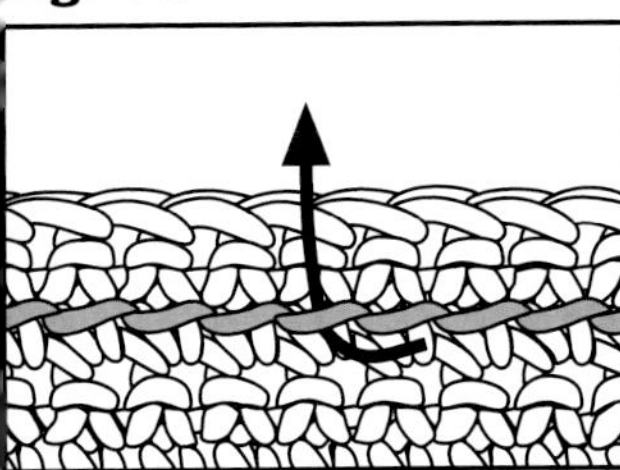

Fig. 4b

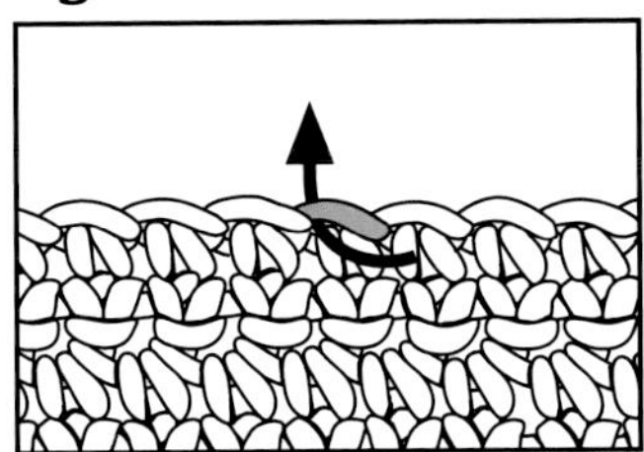

POST STITCH

Work around post of stitch indicated, inserting hook in direction of arrow *(Fig. 5)*.

Fig. 5

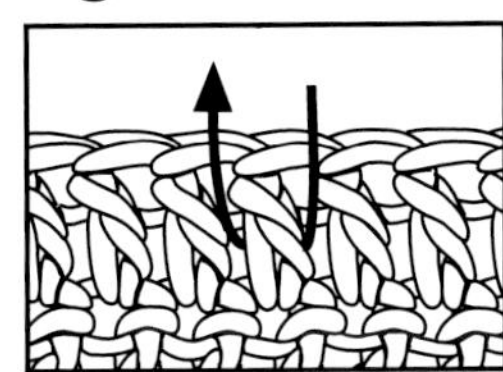

FRINGE

Cut a piece of cardboard 3" wide and ½" longer than you want your finished fringe to be. Wind the yarn **loosely** and **evenly** around the cardboard lengthwise until the card is filled, then cut across one end; repeat as needed.

Hold together half as many strands of yarn as desired for the finished fringe; fold in half.

With **wrong** side facing and using a crochet hook, draw the folded end up through a stitch and pull the loose ends through the folded end *(Fig. 6a)*; draw the knot up **tightly** *(Fig. 6b)*. Repeat, spacing as desired.

Lay flat on a hard surface and trim the ends.

Fig. 6a

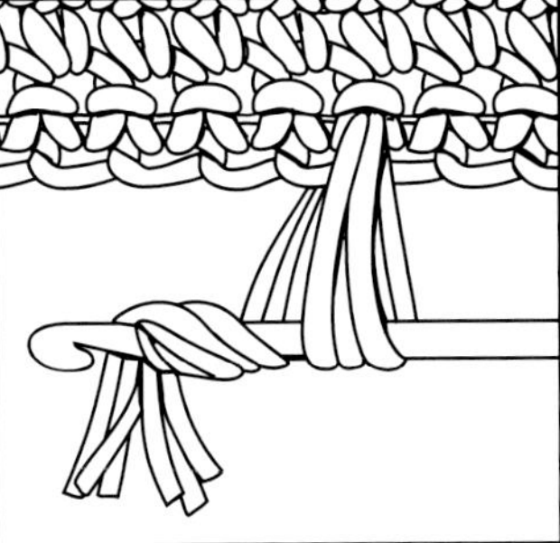

Fig. 6b

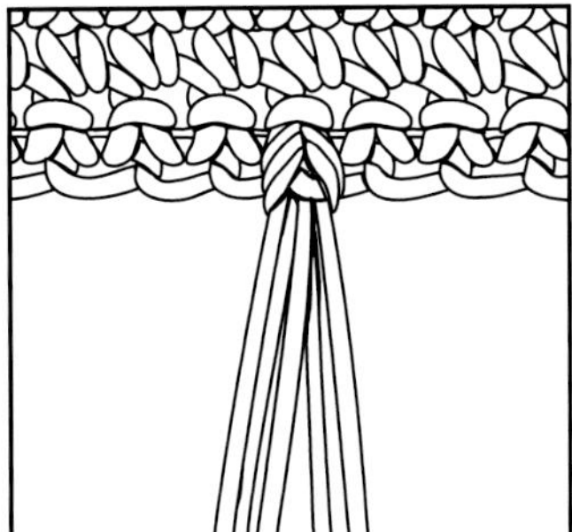

WHIPSTITCH

Place two pieces with **wrong** sides together. Sew through both pieces once to secure the beginning of the seam, leaving an ample yarn end to weave in later. Working through **both** loops on **both** pieces *(Fig. 7a)* **or** through **inside** loop of each stitch on **both** pieces *(Fig. 7b)*, ★ insert the needle from front to back through next stitch and pull yarn through; repeat from ★ across.

Fig. 7a

Fig. 7b

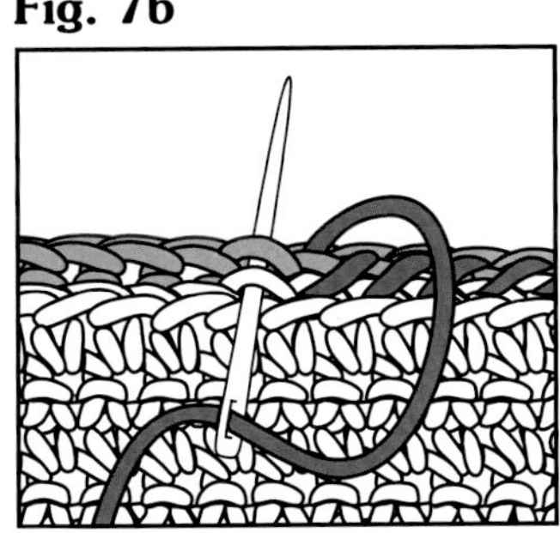

WEAVING SEAMS

With the **right** side of both pieces facing you and edges even, sew through both sides once to secure the beginning of the seam, leaving an ample yarn end to weave in later. Insert the needle from **right** to **left** through one strand on each piece *(Fig. 8)*. Bring the needle around and insert it from **right** to **left** through the next strand on both pieces. Repeat along the edge, being careful to match stitches and rows.

Fig. 8

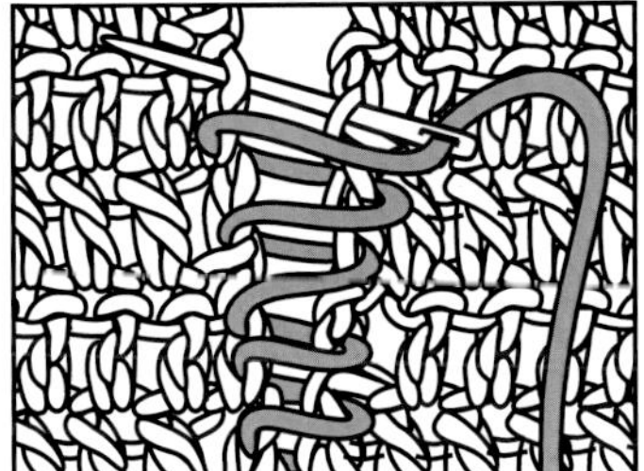

YARN INFORMATION

For your convenience, llisted below is the specific yarn style and colors used to create our photography model. Because yarn manufacturers make frequent changes in their product lines, you may sometimes find it necessary to use a substitute yarn or to search for the discontinued product at alternate suppliers (locally or online).

JANUARY
Wintuk® Yarn
#3001 White
#3025 Baby Pink
#3026 Baby Blue

FEBRUARY
Red Heart® Baby Pompadour
#1001 White
#1722 Light Pink

MARCH
Red Heart® Baby Fingering Weight
#1680 Pastel Green

APRIL
Wendy Peter Pan
#300 White
#306 Blue
#305 Pink
#303 Yellow
#307 Lavender

MAY
Red Heart® Baby Sport Pompadour
#1001 White
#1234 Yellow
#1802 Blue

JUNE
Red Heart® Baby Sport Pompadour
#1001 White
#1680 Pastel Green
#1802 Baby Blue
#1224 Yellow
#1722 Light Pink
#1247 Peach

JULY
Red Heart® Baby Sport Pompadour
#1001 White
#1680 Pastel Green
#1802 Baby Blue

AUGUST
Red Heart® Baby Sport Pompadour
#1001 White
#1384 Skipper Blue
#31324 Bright Yellow

SEPTEMBER
Caron® Cuddlesoft®
#2853 Angel Blue

OCTOBER
Caron® Cuddlesoft®
#2801 White
#2804 Pretty Pansy
#2853 Angel Blue
#2806 Rosy Cheeks
#2850 Cool Mint

NOVEMBER
Caron® Cuddlesoft®
#2801 White
#2853 Angel Blue
#2806 Rosy Cheeks
#2850 Cool Mint
#2804 Pretty Pansy

DECEMBER
Lion Brand® Jamie Baby®
#200 White
#201 Pink
#206 Pastel Blue
#299 Fisherman

We have made every effort to ensure that these instructions are accurate and complete. We cannot, however, be responsible for human error, typographical mistakes, or variations in individual work.

Afghans made and instructions tested by Janet Akins, Belinda Baxter, Marianna Crowder, Freda Gillham, Jo Ann Gonyea, Kathleen Hardy, Shala Johnson, Pat Little, Kay Meadors, Dale Potter, Carla Rains, and Carol Thompson.